Row 31: K2, (YO, slip 1 as if to **knit**, K1, PSSO) twice, ★ K4, (YO, slip 1 as if to **knit**, K1, PSSO) twice; repeat from ★ across to last 2 sts, K2.

Row 33: K3, YO, slip 1 as if to **knit**, K1, PSSO, (K6, YO, slip 1 as if to **knit**, K1, PSSO) across to last 3 sts, K3.

Row 35: Knit across.

Row 37: ★ K1, YO, K3, pass 3rd st on right needle over first 2 sts; repeat from ★ across.

Row 39: Knit across.

Row 41: Knit across.

Row 43: Knit across.

Row 45: ★ SSK (*Figs. 6a-c, page 22*), K 16, K2 tog (*Fig. 4, page 21*); repeat from ★ once **more**: 36 sts.

Row 47: (SSK, K 14, K2 tog) twice: 32 sts.

Row 49: (SSK, K 12, K2 tog) twice: 28 sts.

Row 51: (SSK, K 10, K2 tog) twice: 24 sts.

Row 53: (SSK, K8, K2 tog) twice: 20 sts.

Row 55: K2 tog across: 10 sts.

Row 56: Purl across.

Cut yarn leaving a long end for sewing. Thread yarn needle with end and weave through remaining sts twice, pulling tightly to close; secure end but do **not** cut yarn.

THUMB
Row 1 (Right side)**:** Slip sts from st holder onto larger size needle and knit across: 15 sts.

Row 2: P6, P2 tog (*Fig. 5, page 21*), P7: 14 sts.

Row 3: Knit across.

Row 4: Purl across.

Rows 5-10: Repeat Rows 3 and 4, 3 times.

Row 11: K2 tog across: 7 sts.

Cut yarn leaving a long end for sewing. Thread yarn needle with end and weave through remaining sts twice, pulling tightly to close; secure end and sew Thumb seam.

With remaining ends, sew side seam.

SOAP SACK
With larger size needles, cast on 64 sts.

Row 1 (Right side)**:** Knit across.

Row 2: Purl across.

Rows 3-6: Repeat Rows 1 and 2 twice.

Row 7: K2 tog across: 32 sts.

Row 8: Purl across.

Row 9 (Eyelet row)**:** K1, (YO, K2 tog) across to last st, K1.

Row 10: Purl across.

Row 11: Knit across.

Rows 12-18: Repeat Rows 10 and 11, 3 times; then repeat Row 10 once **more**.

Row 19: ★ K1, YO, K3, pass 3rd st on right needle over first 2 sts; repeat from ★ across.

Row 20 AND ALL EVEN-NUMBERED ROWS:
Purl across.

Instructions continued on page 3.

D1560488

Row 21: Knit across.

Row 23: K3, YO, slip 1 as if to **knit**, K1, PSSO, (K6, YO, slip 1 as if to **knit**, K1, PSSO) across to last 3 sts, K3.

Row 25: K2, (YO, slip 1 as if to **knit**, K1, PSSO) twice, ★ K4, (YO, slip 1 as if to **knit**, K1, PSSO) twice; repeat from ★ 2 times **more**, K2.

Row 27: K1, (YO, slip 1 as if to **knit**, K1, PSSO) 3 times, ★ K2, (YO, slip 1 as if to **knit**, K1, PSSO) 3 times; repeat from ★ 2 times **more**, K1.

Row 29: K2, (YO, slip 1 as if to **knit**, K1, PSSO) twice, ★ K4, (YO, slip 1 as if to **knit**, K1, PSSO) twice; repeat from ★ 2 times **more**, K2.

Row 31: K3, YO, slip 1 as if to **knit**, K1, PSSO, (K6, YO, slip 1 as if to **knit**, K1, PSSO) across to last 3 sts, K3.

Row 33: Knit across.

Row 35: ★ K1, YO, K3, pass 3rd st on right needle over first 2 sts; repeat from ★ across.

Rows 36-42: Repeat Rows 10 and 11, 3 times; then repeat Row 10 once **more**.

Row 43: K2 tog across: 16 sts.

Cut yarn leaving a long end for sewing. Thread yarn needle with end and weave through remaining sts twice, pulling tightly to close; secure end and sew seam.

Weave ribbon through Eyelet row or crochet an 18" (45.5 cm) chain and weave through Eyelet row.

FACECLOTH
With larger size needles, cast on 38 sts.

Rows 1-5: Knit across.

Row 6: K3, P 32, K3.

Row 7 (Right side)**:** Knit across.

Rows 8-20: Repeat Rows 6 and 7, 6 times; then repeat Row 6 once **more**.

Row 21: K4, YO, K3, pass 3rd st on right needle over first 2 sts, ★ K1, YO, K3, pass 3rd st on right needle over first 2 sts; repeat from ★ across to last 3 sts, K3.

Row 22 AND ALL EVEN-NUMBERED ROWS: K3, P 32, K3.

Row 23: Knit across.

Row 25: K6, (YO, slip 1 as if to **knit**, K1, PSSO, K6) across.

Row 27: K5, (YO, slip 1 as if to **knit**, K1, PSSO) twice, ★ K4, (YO, slip 1 as if to **knit**, K1, PSSO) twice; repeat from ★ 2 times **more**, K5.

Row 29: K4, (YO, slip 1 as if to **knit**, K1, PSSO) 3 times, ★ K2, (YO, slip 1 as if to **knit**, K1, PSSO) 3 times; repeat from ★ 2 times **more**, K4.

Row 31: K5, (YO, slip 1 as if to **knit**, K1, PSSO) twice, ★ K4, (YO, slip 1 as if to **knit**, K1, PSSO) twice; repeat from ★ 2 times **more**, K5.

Row 33: K6, (YO, slip 1 as if to **knit**, K1, PSSO, K6) across.

Row 35: Knit across.

Row 37: K4, YO, K3, pass 3rd st on right needle over first 2 sts, ★ K1, YO, K3, pass 3rd st on right needle over first 2 sts; repeat from ★ across to last 3 sts, K3.

Rows 38-53: Repeat Rows 22 and 23, 8 times.

Rows 54-57: Knit across.

Bind off all sts in **knit**.

PARADISE ▰▰▱▱ EASY

Shown on page 12.

Finished Sizes

Bath Mitt: Adult size
Soap Sack: 7" (18 cm) circumference x 6¹⁄₂" (16.5 cm) tall
Facecloth: 8¹⁄₄"w (21 cm) x 8³⁄₄"h (22 cm)

MATERIALS

100% Cotton Medium/Worsted Weight Yarn
  [2¹⁄₂ ounces, 120 yards
  (70.9 grams, 110 meters) per skein]: 2 skeins
Knitting needles, sizes 5 (3.75 mm) **and** 7 (4.5 mm)
  or sizes needed for gauge
Markers
Stitch holder
Yarn needle
¹⁄₄"w (7 mm) Ribbon - 18" (45.5 cm) length **or**
  size G (4 mm) crochet hook (for chain)

GAUGE: In Stockinette Stitch,
    17 sts and 26 rows = 4" (10 cm)

BATH MITT
RIBBING

With smaller size needles, cast on 39 sts.

Row 1: P1, (K1, P1) across.

Row 2: K1, (P1, K1) across.

Rows 3-12: Repeat Rows 1 and 2, 5 times.

BODY

Change to larger size needles.

Row 1 (Right side)**:** Knit across.

Row 2: Purl across.

Row 3: K3, YO (*Fig. 2a, page 21*), [slip 1 as if to **knit**, K1, PSSO (*Figs. 7a & b, page 22*)], (K6, YO, slip 1 as if to **knit**, K1, PSSO) across to last 2 sts, K2.

Row 4 AND ALL EVEN-NUMBERED ROWS THROUGH Row 22: Purl across.

Row 5: K2, YO, [slip 1 as if to **knit**, K2 tog, PSSO (*Fig. 8, page 22*)], (YO, K5, YO, slip 1 as if to **knit**, K2 tog, PSSO) across to last 2 sts, YO, K2.

Row 7: K3, YO, slip 1 as if to **knit**, K1, PSSO, (K6, YO, slip 1 as if to **knit**, K1, PSSO) across to last 2 sts, K2.

Row 9: K 19, place marker (*see Markers, page 20*), M1 (*Figs. 3a & b, page 21*), K1, M1, place marker, knit across: 41 sts.

Row 11: K7, YO, slip 1 as if to **knit**, K1, PSSO, K6, YO, slip 1 as if to **knit**, K1, PSSO, K2, slip next marker, M1, K3, M1, slip next marker, K3, (YO, slip 1 as if to **knit**, K1, PSSO, K6) twice: 43 sts.

Row 13: K6, YO, slip 1 as if to **knit**, K2 tog, PSSO, YO, K5, YO, slip 1 as if to **knit**, K2 tog, PSSO, YO, K2, slip next marker, M1, K5, M1, slip next marker, K2, YO, slip 1 as if to **knit**, K2 tog, PSSO, YO, K5, YO, slip 1 as if to **knit**, K2 tog, PSSO, YO, K6: 45 sts.

Row 15: K7, YO, slip 1 as if to **knit**, K1, PSSO, K6, YO, slip 1 as if to **knit**, K1, PSSO, K2, slip next marker, M1, K7, M1, slip next marker, K3, (YO, slip 1 as if to **knit**, K1, PSSO, K6) twice: 47 sts.

Row 17: Knit across to next marker, slip marker, M1, K9, M1, slip next marker, knit across: 49 sts.

Instructions continued on page 5.

Row 19: K3, (YO, slip 1 as if to **knit**, K1, PSSO, K6) twice, slip next marker, M1, K 11, M1, slip next marker, K7, YO, slip 1 as if to **knit**, K1, PSSO, K6, YO, slip 1 as if to **knit**, K1, PSSO, K2: 51 sts.

Row 21: K2, YO, slip 1 as if to **knit**, K2 tog, PSSO, YO, K5, YO, slip 1 as if to **knit**, K2 tog, PSSO, YO, K6, slip next marker, M1, K 13, M1, slip next marker, K6, YO, slip 1 as if to **knit**, K2 tog, PSSO, YO, K5, YO, slip 1 as if to **knit**, K2 tog, PSSO, YO, K2: 53 sts.

Row 23: K3, (YO, slip 1 as if to **knit**, K1, PSSO, K6) twice, remove next marker, place next 15 sts onto st holder, remove next marker, K7, YO, slip 1 as if to **knit**, K1, PSSO, K6, YO, slip 1 as if to **knit**, K1, PSSO, K2: 38 sts.

Row 24: Purl across.

Row 25: Knit across.

Rows 26-37: Repeat Rows 24 and 25, 6 times.

Row 38: P 19, place marker, P 19.

Row 39 (Decrease row): SSK *(Figs. 6a-c, page 22)*, knit across to within 2 sts of marker, K2 tog *(Fig. 4, page 21)*, SSK, knit across to last 2 sts, K2 tog: 34 sts.

Row 40: Purl across.

Rows 41-48: Repeat Rows 39 and 40, 4 times: 18 sts.

Row 49: K2 tog across: 9 sts.

Row 50: Purl across.

Cut yarn leaving a long end for sewing. Thread yarn needle with end and weave through remaining sts twice, pulling tightly to close; secure end but do **not** cut yarn.

THUMB

Row 1 (Right side): Slip sts from st holder onto larger size needle and knit across: 15 sts.

Row 2: P6, P2 tog *(Fig. 5, page 21)*, P7: 14 sts.

Row 3: Knit across.

Row 4: Purl across.

Rows 5-10: Repeat Rows 3 and 4, 3 times.

Row 11: K2 tog across: 7 sts.

Cut yarn leaving a long end for sewing. Thread yarn needle with end and weave through remaining sts twice, pulling tightly to close; secure end and sew Thumb seam.

With remaining ends, sew side seam.

SOAP SACK

With larger size needles, cast on 62 sts.

Row 1 (Right side): Knit across.

Row 2: Purl across.

Rows 3-6: Repeat Rows 1 and 2 twice.

Row 7: K2 tog across: 31 sts.

Row 8: Purl across.

Row 9: Knit across.

Row 10: Purl across.

Row 11 (Eyelet row): K1, (YO, K2 tog) across.

Rows 12-17: Repeat Rows 8 and 9, 3 times.

Row 18 AND ALL EVEN-NUMBERED ROWS THROUGH Row 30: Purl across.

Row 19: K3, YO, slip 1 as if to **knit**, K1, PSSO, (K6, YO, slip 1 as if to **knit**, K1, PSSO) across to last 2 sts, K2.

Row 21: K2, YO, slip 1 as if to **knit**, K2 tog, PSSO, (YO, K5, YO, slip 1 as if to **knit**, K2 tog, PSSO) across to last 2 sts, YO, K2.

Row 23: K3, YO, slip 1 as if to **knit**, K1, PSSO, (K6, YO, slip 1 as if to **knit**, K1, PSSO) across to last 2 sts, K2.

Row 25: Knit across.

Row 27: K7, (YO, slip 1 as if to **knit**, K1, PSSO, K6) across.

Row 29: K6, YO, slip 1 as if to **knit**, K2 tog, PSSO, (YO, K5, YO, slip 1 as if to **knit**, K2 tog, PSSO) twice, YO, K6.

Row 31: K7, (YO, slip 1 as if to **knit**, K1, PSSO, K6) across.

Rows 32-40: Repeat Rows 8 and 9, 4 times; then repeat Row 8 once **more**.

Row 41: K1, K2 tog across: 16 sts.

Cut yarn leaving a long end for sewing. Thread yarn needle with end and weave through remaining sts twice, pulling tightly to close; secure end and sew seam.

Weave ribbon through Eyelet row or crochet an 18" (45.5 cm) chain and weave through Eyelet row.

FACECLOTH

With larger size needles, cast on 37 sts.

Rows 1-4: K1, (P1, K1) across.

Row 5 (Right side)**:** K1, P1, K 33, P1, K1.

Row 6 AND ALL EVEN-NUMBERED ROWS: K1, P1, K1, P 31, K1, P1, K1.

Row 7: K1, P1, K4, YO, slip 1 as if to **knit**, K1, PSSO, (K6, YO, slip 1 as if to **knit**, K1, PSSO) across to last 5 sts, K3, P1, K1.

Row 9: K1, P1, K3, YO, slip 1 as if to **knit**, K2 tog, PSSO, (YO, K5, YO, slip 1 as if to **knit**, K2 tog, PSSO) across to last 5 sts, YO, K3, P1, K1.

Row 11: K1, P1, K4, YO, slip 1 as if to **knit**, K1, PSSO, (K6, YO, slip 1 as if to **knit**, K1, PSSO) across to last 5 sts, K3, P1, K1.

Row 13: K1, P1, K 33, P1, K1.

Row 15: K1, P1, K8, YO, slip 1 as if to **knit**, K1, PSSO, (K6, YO, slip 1 as if to **knit**, K1, PSSO) twice, K7, P1, K1.

Row 17: K1, P1, K7, YO, slip 1 as if to **knit**, K2 tog, PSSO, (YO, K5, YO, slip 1 as if to **knit**, K2 tog, PSSO) twice, YO, K7, P1, K1.

Row 19: K1, P1, K8, YO, slip 1 as if to **knit**, K1, PSSO, (K6, YO, slip 1 as if to **knit**, K1, PSSO) twice, K7, P1, K1.

Row 21: K1, P1, K 33, P1, K1.

Rows 22-52: Repeat Rows 6-21 once, then repeat Rows 6-20 once **more**.

Rows 53-56: K1, (P1, K1) across.

Bind off all sts in **knit**.

REJUVENATE

Shown on page 10.

Finished Sizes
Bath Mitt: Adult size
Soap Sack: 6" (15 cm) circumference x 5³/₄" (14.5 cm) tall
Facecloth: 8¹/₂"w (21.5 cm) x 9"h (23 cm)

MATERIALS
100% Cotton Medium/Worsted Weight Yarn
   [2¹/₂ ounces, 120 yards
   (70.9 grams, 110 meters) per skein]: 2 skeins
Knitting needles, sizes 5 (3.75 mm) **and** 7 (4.5 mm)
   or sizes needed for gauge
Markers
Stitch holder
Yarn needle
¹/₄"w (7 mm) Ribbon - 42" (106.5 cm) length **or**
   size G (4 mm) crochet hook (for chain)

GAUGE: In Stockinette Stitch,
       17 sts and 26 rows = 4" (10 cm)

STITCH GUIDE

KNOT ST (uses 3 sts)
P3 tog but do **not** drop sts off left needle, knit **same** 3 sts on left needle together but do **not** drop sts off left needle, purl **same** 3 sts on left needle together dropping 3 sts off left needle.

BATH MITT
CUFF
With smaller size needles, cast on 82 sts.

Row 1 (Right side)**:** Knit across.

Row 2: Purl across.

Rows 3-6: Repeat Rows 1 and 2 twice.

Row 7: K2 tog across (*Fig. 4, page 21*): 41 sts.

Row 8: Purl across.

Row 9 (Eyelet row)**:** K1, ★ YO (*Fig. 2a, page 21*), K2 tog; repeat from ★ across.

BODY
Change to larger size needles.

Row 1: Purl across.

Row 2: Knit across.

Rows 3-9: Repeat Rows 1 and 2, 3 times; then repeat Row 1 once **more**.

Row 10: K3, work Knot St, (K5, work Knot St) across to last 3 sts, K3.

Rows 11-15: Repeat Rows 1 and 2 twice, then repeat Row 1 once **more**.

Row 16: K7, work Knot St, (K5, work Knot St) 3 times, K7.

Row 17 AND ALL ODD-NUMBERED ROWS: Purl across.

Row 18: K 20, place marker (*see Markers, page 20*), M1 (*Figs. 3a & b, page 21*), K1, M1, place marker, knit across: 43 sts.

Row 20: Knit across to next marker, slip marker, M1, K3, M1, slip next marker, knit across: 45 sts.

Row 22: K3, work Knot St, K5, work Knot St, K6, slip next marker, M1, K5, M1, slip next marker, K6, work Knot St, K5, work Knot St, K3: 47 sts.

Row 24: Knit across to next marker, slip marker, M1, K7, M1, slip next marker, knit across: 49 sts.

Row 26: Knit across to next marker, slip marker, M1, K9, M1, slip next marker, knit across: 51 sts.

Row 28: K7, work Knot St, K5, work Knot St, K2, slip next marker, M1, K 11, M1, slip next marker, K2, work Knot St, K5, work Knot St, K7: 53 sts.

Row 30: Knit across to next marker, slip marker, M1, K 13, M1, slip next marker, knit across: 55 sts.

Row 32: Knit across to next marker, remove marker, slip next 15 sts onto st holder, remove next marker, knit across: 40 sts.

Row 34: K3, work Knot St, K5, work Knot St, K 12, work Knot St, K5, work Knot St, K3.

Row 36: Knit across.

Row 38: Knit across.

Row 40: K7, work Knot St, K5, work Knot St, K4, work Knot St, K5, work Knot St, K7.

Row 42: Knit across.

Row 44: Knit across.

Row 46: K3, work Knot St, K5, work Knot St, K 12, work Knot St, K5, work Knot St, K3.

Row 48: ★ SSK *(Figs. 6a-c, page 22)*, K 16, K2 tog; repeat from ★ once **more**: 36 sts.

Row 50: (SSK, K 14, K2 tog) twice: 32 sts.

Row 52: (SSK, K 12, K2 tog) twice: 28 sts.

Row 54: (SSK, K 10, K2 tog) twice: 24 sts.

Row 56: (SSK, K8, K2 tog) twice: 20 sts.

Row 58: K2 tog across: 10 sts.

Row 59: Purl across.

Cut yarn leaving a long end for sewing. Thread yarn needle with end and weave through remaining sts twice, pulling tightly to close; secure end but do **not** cut yarn.

THUMB

Row 1 (Right side)**:** Slip sts from st holder onto larger size needle and knit across: 15 sts.

Row 2: P6, P2 tog *(Fig. 5, page 21)*, P7: 14 sts.

Row 3: Knit across.

Row 4: Purl across.

Rows 5-10: Repeat Rows 3 and 4, 3 times.

Row 11: K2 tog across: 7 sts.

Cut yarn leaving a long end for sewing. Thread yarn needle with end and weave through remaining sts twice, pulling tightly to close; secure end and sew Thumb seam.

With remaining ends, sew side seam.

Weave a 24" (61 cm) length of ribbon through Eyelet row or crochet a 24" (61 cm) chain and weave through Eyelet row.

Instructions continued on page 9.

SOAP SACK

With larger size needles, cast on 15 sts.

Row 1 (Right side): K1, increase in each st across *(Figs. 1a & b, page 21)*: 29 sts.

Row 2: Purl across.

Row 3: Knit across.

Rows 4-6: Repeat Rows 2 and 3 once, then repeat Row 2 once **more**.

Row 7: K5, (work Knot St, K5) across.

Rows 8-12: Repeat Rows 2 and 3 twice, then repeat Row 2 once **more**.

Row 13: K9, work Knot St, K5, work Knot St, K9.

Rows 14-42: Repeat Rows 2-13 twice, then repeat Rows 2-6 once **more**.

Row 43 (Eyelet row): K1, (YO, K2 tog) across to last 2 sts, K2.

Row 44: Purl across.

Row 45: K1, (increase, K1) across: 43 sts.

Rows 46-48: Repeat Rows 2 and 3 once, then repeat Row 2 once **more**.

Bind off all sts in **knit**, leaving a long end for sewing.

Thread yarn needle with end and sew seam; weave yarn through cast on edge, gather tightly and secure end.

Weave an 18" (45.5 cm) length of ribbon through Eyelet row or crochet an 18" (45.5 cm) chain and weave through Eyelet row.

FACECLOTH

With larger size needles, cast on 39 sts.

Rows 1-4: K1, (P1, K1) across.

Row 5 (Right side): K1, P1, K 35, P1, K1.

Row 6: K1, P1, K1, P 33, K1, P1, K1.

Rows 7-10: Repeat Rows 5 and 6 twice.

Row 11: K1, P1, K4, work Knot St, (K5, work Knot St) 3 times, K4, P1, K1.

Rows 12-16: Repeat Rows 6-10.

Row 17: K1, P1, K8, work Knot St, (K5, work Knot St) twice, K8, P1, K1.

Rows 18-52: Repeat Rows 6-17 twice, then repeat Rows 6-16 once **more**.

Rows 53-56: K1, (P1, K1) across.

Bind off all sts in **knit**.

SUNRAYS

EASY

Shown on page 13.

Finished Sizes

Bath Mitt: Adult size

Soap Sack: 6" (15 cm) circumference x 5³/₄" (14.5 cm) tall

Facecloth: 8"w (20.5 cm) x 8³/₄"h (22 cm)

MATERIALS

100% Cotton Medium/Worsted Weight Yarn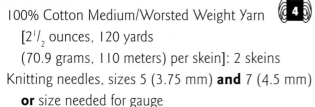
[2¹/₂ ounces, 120 yards
(70.9 grams, 110 meters) per skein]: 2 skeins
Knitting needles, sizes 5 (3.75 mm) **and** 7 (4.5 mm)
  or size needed for gauge
Markers
Stitch holder
Yarn needle
¹/₄"w (7 mm) Ribbon - 18" (45.5 cm) length **or**
  size G (4 mm) crochet hook (for chain)

GAUGE: In Stockinette Stitch,
     17 sts and 26 rows = 4" (10 cm)

BATH MITT
CUFF

With smaller size needles, cast on 39 sts.

Row 1: Knit across.

Row 2: K1, P2, ★ slip 1 as if to **knit**, K2, PSSO *(Fig. A)*, P2; repeat from ★ across to last st, K1: 32 sts.

Fig. A

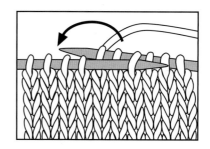

Row 3: P1, K2, ★ P1, YO *(Fig. 2b, page 21)*, P1, K2; repeat from ★ across to last st, P1: 39 sts.

Row 4: K1, P2, (K3, P2) across to last st, K1.

Row 5: P1, K2, (P3, K2) across to last st, P1.

Rows 6-15: Repeat Rows 2-5 twice, then repeat Rows 2 and 3 once **more**: 39 sts.

BODY

Change to larger size needles.

Row 1 (Right side)**:** Knit across.

Row 2: Purl across.

Rows 3-6: Repeat Rows 1 and 2 twice.

Row 7: K 19, place marker *(see Markers, page 20)*, M1 *(Figs. 3a & b, page 21)*, K1, M1, place marker, knit across: 41 sts.

Instructions continued on page 15.

Row 8 AND ALL EVEN-NUMBERED ROWS: Purl across.

Row 9: Knit across to next marker, slip marker, M1, K3, M1, slip next marker, knit across: 43 sts.

Row 11: Knit across to next marker, slip marker, M1, K5, M1, slip next marker, knit across: 45 sts.

Row 13: Knit across to next marker, slip marker, M1, K7, M1, slip next marker, knit across: 47 sts.

Row 15: Knit across to next marker, slip marker, M1, K9, M1, slip next marker, knit across: 49 sts.

Row 17: Knit across to next marker, slip marker, M1, K11, M1, slip next marker, knit across: 51 sts.

Row 19: Knit across to next marker, slip marker, M1, K13, M1, slip next marker, knit across: 53 sts.

Row 21: Knit across to next marker, remove marker, slip next 15 sts onto st holder, remove next marker, knit across: 38 sts.

Row 23: Knit across.

Row 25: Knit across.

Row 27: Knit across.

Row 29: Knit across.

Row 31: Knit across.

Row 33: Knit across.

Row 35: Knit across.

Row 37: Knit across.

Row 39: Knit across.

Row 41: ★ SSK *(Figs. 6a-c, page 22)*, K15, K2 tog *(Fig. 4, page 21)*; repeat from ★ once **more**: 34 sts.

Row 43: (SSK, K13, K2 tog) twice: 30 sts.

Row 45: (SSK, K11, K2 tog) twice: 26 sts.

Row 47: (SSK, K9, K2 tog) twice: 22 sts.

Row 49: (SSK, K7, K2 tog) twice: 18 sts.

Row 51: K2 tog across: 9 sts.

Row 52: Purl across.

Cut yarn leaving a long end for sewing. Thread yarn needle with end and weave through remaining sts twice, pulling tightly to close; secure end but do **not** cut yarn.

THUMB

Row 1 (Right side)**:** Slip sts from st holder onto larger size needle and knit across: 15 sts.

Row 2: P6, P2 tog *(Fig. 5, page 21)*, P7: 14 sts.

Row 3: Knit across.

Row 4: Purl across.

Rows 5-10: Repeat Rows 3 and 4, 3 times.

Row 11: K2 tog across: 7 sts.

Cut yarn leaving a long end for sewing. Thread yarn needle with end and weave through remaining sts twice, pulling tightly to close; secure end and sew Thumb seam.

With remaining ends, sew side seam.

SOAP SACK

With larger size needles, cast on 16 sts.

Row 1 (Right side): Increase in each st across (*Figs. 1a & b, page 21*): 32 sts.

Row 2: K2, (P3, K2) across.

Row 3: P2, (slip 1 as if to **knit**, K2, PSSO, P2) across: 26 sts.

Row 4: K2, (P1, YO, P1, K2) across: 32 sts.

Row 5: P2, (K3, P2) across.

Rows 6-30: Repeat Rows 2-5, 6 times; then repeat Row 2 once **more**.

Row 31 (Eyelet row): K2, (YO, K2 tog) across to last 2 sts, K2.

Row 32: Purl across.

Row 33: Increase in each st across: 64 sts.

Row 34: Purl across.

Row 35: Knit across.

Row 36: Purl across.

Bind off all sts in **knit**, leaving a long end for sewing.

Thread yarn needle with end and sew seam; weave yarn through cast on edge, gather tightly and secure end.

Weave an 18" (45.5 cm) length of ribbon through Eyelet row or crochet an 18" (45.5 cm) chain and weave through Eyelet row.

FACECLOTH

With larger size needles, cast on 42 sts.

Row 1: Knit across.

Row 2 (Right side): P2, (slip 1 as if to **knit**, K2, PSSO, P2) across: 34 sts.

Row 3: K2, (P1, YO, P1, K2) across: 42 sts.

Row 4: P2, (K3, P2) across.

Row 5: K2, (P3, K2) across.

Rows 6-12: Repeat Rows 2-5 once, then repeat Rows 2-4 once **more**.

Row 13: (K2, P3) twice, K 22, (P3, K2) twice.

Row 14: P2, (slip 1 as if to **knit**, K2, PSSO, P2) twice, K 18, P2, (slip 1 as if to **knit**, K2, PSSO, P2) twice: 38 sts.

Row 15: K2, (P1, YO, P1, K2) twice, K1, P 16, K3, (P1, YO, P1, K2) twice: 42 sts.

Row 16: P2, (K3, P2) twice, K 18, P2, (K3, P2) twice.

Row 17: (K2, P3) twice, K3, P 16, K3, (P3, K2) twice.

Rows 18-44: Repeat Rows 14-17, 6 times; then repeat Rows 14-16 once **more**.

Row 45: (K2, P3) twice, K 22, (P3, K2) twice.

Rows 46-58: Repeat Rows 2-5, 3 times; then repeat Row 2 once **more**.

Bind off all sts in **knit**.

TRANQUILITY

●■□□ EASY

Shown on Front Cover.

Finished Sizes
Bath Mitt: Adult size
Soap Sack: 6" (15 cm) circumference x 6" (15 cm) tall
Facecloth: 9" (23 cm) square

MATERIALS

100% Cotton Medium/Worsted Weight Yarn
  [2$\frac{1}{2}$ ounces, 120 yards
  (70.9 grams, 110 meters) per skein]: 2 skeins
Knitting needles, sizes 5 (3.75 mm) **and** 7 (4.5 mm)
  or sizes needed for gauge
Markers
Stitch holder
Yarn needle
$\frac{1}{4}$"w (7 mm) Ribbon - 42" (106.5 cm) length **or**
  size G (4 mm) crochet hook (for chain)

GAUGE: In Stockinette Stitch,
          17 sts and 26 rows = 4" (10 cm)

BATH MITT
CUFF

With smaller size needles, cast on 80 sts.

Row 1 (Right side): Knit across.

Row 2: Purl across.

Rows 3-6: Repeat Rows 1 and 2 twice.

Row 7: K2 tog across (*Fig. 4, page 21*): 40 sts.

Row 8: Purl across.

Row 9 (Eyelet row): K1, ★ YO (*Fig. 2a, page 21*), K2 tog; repeat from ★ across to last st, K1.

BODY
Change to larger size needles.

Row 1 AND ALL ODD-NUMBERED ROWS: Purl across.

Row 2: K7, (K2 tog, YO) 3 times, knit across.

Row 4: K8, (K2 tog, YO) twice, knit across.

Row 6: K7, (K2 tog, YO) 3 times, knit across.

Row 8: K8, (K2 tog, YO) twice, knit across.

Row 10: K7, (K2 tog, YO) 3 times, knit across.

Row 12: K8, (K2 tog, YO) twice, K8, increase (*Figs. 1a & b, page 21*), knit across: 41 sts.

Row 14: K7, (K2, tog, YO) 3 times, K7, place marker (*see Markers, page 20*), M1 (*Figs. 3a & b, page 21*), K1, M1, place marker, knit across: 43 sts.

Row 16: K8, (K2 tog, YO) twice, K8, slip next marker, M1, K3, M1, slip next marker, knit across: 45 sts.

Row 18: K7, (K2 tog, YO) 3 times, K7, slip next marker, M1, K5, M1, slip next marker, knit across: 47 sts.

Row 20: K8, (K2 tog, YO) twice, K8, slip next marker, M1, K7, M1, slip next marker, knit across: 49 sts.

Row 22: K7, (K2 tog, YO) 3 times, K7, slip next marker, M1, K9, M1, slip next marker, knit across: 51 sts.

Row 24: K8, (K2 tog, YO) twice, K8, slip next marker, M1, K11, M1, slip next marker, knit across: 53 sts.

Row 26: K7, (K2 tog, YO) 3 times, K7, slip next marker, M1, K13, M1, slip next marker, knit across: 55 sts.

Row 28: K8, (K2 tog, YO) twice, K8, remove next marker, slip next 15 sts onto st holder, remove next marker, knit across: 40 sts.

Row 30: K7, (K2 tog, YO) 3 times, knit across.

Row 32: K8, (K2 tog, YO) twice, knit across.

Rows 34-47: Repeat Rows 30-33, 3 times; then repeat Rows 30 and 31 once **more**.

Row 48: SSK *(Figs. 6a-c, page 22)*, K6, (K2 tog, YO) twice, K6, K2 tog, SSK, K 16, K2 tog: 36 sts.

Row 50: SSK, K4, (K2 tog, YO) 3 times, K4, K2 tog, SSK, K 14, K2 tog: 32 sts.

Row 52: SSK, K4, (K2 tog, YO) twice, K4, K2 tog, SSK, K 12, K2 tog: 28 sts.

Row 54: SSK, K2, (K2 tog, YO) 3 times, K2, K2 tog, SSK, K 10, K2 tog: 24 sts.

Row 56: K2 tog across: 12 sts.

Row 57: Purl across.

Cut yarn leaving a long end for sewing. Thread yarn needle with end and weave through remaining sts twice, pulling tightly to close; secure end but do **not** cut yarn.

THUMB
Row 1 (Right side)**:** Slip sts from st holder onto larger size needle and knit across: 15 sts.

Row 2: P6, P2 tog *(Fig. 5, page 21)*, P7: 14 sts.

Row 3: Knit across.

Row 4: Purl across.

Rows 5-10: Repeat Rows 3 and 4, 3 times.

Row 11: K2 tog across: 7 sts.

Cut yarn leaving a long end for sewing. Thread yarn needle with end and weave through remaining sts twice, pulling tightly to close; secure end and sew Thumb seam.

With remaining ends, sew side seam.

Weave a 24" (61 cm) length of ribbon through Eyelet row or crochet a 24" (61 cm) chain and weave through Eyelet row.

SOAP SACK
With larger size needles, cast on 56 sts.

Row 1 (Right side)**:** Knit across.

Row 2: Purl across.

Rows 3 and 4: Repeat Rows 1 and 2.

Row 5: K2 tog across: 28 sts.

Row 6: Purl across.

Row 7 (Eyelet row)**:** K1, (YO, K2 tog) across to last st, K1.

Row 8: Purl across.

Row 9: Knit across.

Row 10: Purl across.

Row 11: K 11, (K2 tog, YO) 3 times, K 11.

Instructions continued on page 19.

Row 12 AND ALL EVEN-NUMBERED ROWS: Purl across.

Row 13: K 12, (K2 tog, YO) twice, K 12.

Row 15: K 11, (K2 tog, YO) 3 times, K 11.

Rows 16-36: Repeat Rows 12-15, 5 times; then repeat Row 12 once **more**.

Row 37: K2 tog across: 14 sts.

Cut yarn leaving a long end for sewing. Thread yarn needle with end and weave through remaining sts twice, pulling tightly to close; secure end and sew seam.

Weave an 18" (45.5 cm) length of ribbon through Eyelet row or crochet an 18" (45.5 cm) chain and weave through Eyelet row.

FACECLOTH

With larger size needles, cast on 39 sts.

Rows 1-5: K1, (P1, K1) across.

Row 6: K1, P1, K1, P 33, K1, P1, K1.

Row 7 (Right side)**:** (K1, P1) twice, K6, (K2 tog, YO) 3 times, K7, (K2 tog, YO) 3 times, K6, (P1, K1) twice.

Row 8: K1, P1, K1, P 33, K1, P1, K1.

Row 9: (K1, P1) twice, K7, (K2 tog, YO) twice, K9, (K2 tog, YO) twice, K7, (P1, K1) twice.

Row 10: K1, P1, K1, P 33, K1, P1, K1.

Rows 11-54: Repeat Rows 7-10, 11 times.

Rows 55-59: K1, (P1, K1) across.

Bind off all sts in **knit**.

HEADBAND

Finished Size: 19" (48.5 cm) circumference

MATERIALS
100% Cotton Medium/Worsted Weight Yarn [2¹/₂ ounces, 120 yards (70.9 grams, 110 meters) per skein]: One skein
Knitting needles, size 7 (4.5 mm) **or** size needed for gauge
Yarn needle

GAUGE: In pattern, 17 sts = 4" (10 cm)

HEADBAND

Cast on 83 sts.

Row 1 (Right side)**:** Knit across.

Row 2: K4, P3, (K5, P3) across to last 4 sts, K4.

Row 3: P4, K3, (P5, K3) across to last 4 sts, P4.

Row 4: K4, P3, (K5, P3) across to last 4 sts, K4.

Row 5: Knit across.

Row 6: P3, (K5, P3) across.

Row 7: K3, (P5, K3) across.

Row 8: P3, (K5, P3) across.

Rows 9-16: Repeat Rows 1-8.

Bind off all sts in **knit**, leaving a long end for sewing.

Sew end of rows together.

GENERAL INSTRUCTIONS

ABBREVIATIONS

cm	centimeters
K	knit
M1	Make One
mm	millimeters
P	purl
PSSO	pass slipped stitch over
SSK	slip, slip, knit
st(s)	stitch(es)
tog	together
YO	yarn over

★ — work instructions following ★ **as many** times as indicated in addition to the first time.

( ) or [ ] — work enclosed instructions **as many** times as specified by the number immediately following **or** contains explanatory remarks.

colon (:) — the number(s) given after a colon at the end of a row or round denote(s) the number of stitches you should have on that row or round.

GAUGE

Exact gauge is **essential** for proper size. Before beginning your project, make a sample swatch in the yarn and needle specified in the individual instructions. After completing the swatch, measure it, counting your stitches and rows carefully. If your swatch is larger or smaller than specified, **make another, changing needle size to get the correct gauge**. Keep trying until you find the size needles that will give you the specified gauge.

MARKERS

As a convenience to you, we have used markers to help distinguish the beginning of a pattern. Place markers as instructed. You may use purchased markers or tie a length of contrasting color yarn around the needle. When you reach a marker on each row, slip it from the left needle to the right needle; remove it when no longer needed.

KNIT TERMINOLOGY	
UNITED STATES	**INTERNATIONAL**
gauge =	tension
bind off =	cast off
yarn over (YO) =	yarn forward (yfwd) **or**
	yarn around needle (yrn)

Yarn Weight Symbol & Names	SUPER FINE 1	FINE 2	LIGHT 3	MEDIUM 4	BULKY 5	SUPER BULKY 6
Type of Yarns in Category	Sock, Fingering Baby	Sport, Baby	DK, Light Worsted	Worsted, Afghan, Aran	Chunky, Craft, Rug	Bulky, Roving
Knit Gauge Ranges in Stockinette St to 4" (10 cm)	27-32 sts	23-26 sts	21-24 sts	16-20 sts	12-15 sts	6-11 sts
Advised Needle Size Range	1-3	3-5	5-7	7-9	9-11	11 and larger

KNITTING NEEDLES															
U.S.	0	1	2	3	4	5	6	7	8	9	10	10½	11	13	15	17
U.K.	13	12	11	10	9	8	7	6	5	4	3	2	1	00	000	---
Metric - mm	2	2.25	2.75	3.25	3.5	3.75	4	4.5	5	5.5	6	6.5	8	9	10	12.75

■□□□ BEGINNER	Projects for first-time knitters using basic knit and purl stitches. Minimal shaping.
■■□□ EASY	Projects using basic stitches, repetitive stitch patterns, simple color changes, and simple shaping and finishing.
■■■□ INTERMEDIATE	Projects with a variety of stitches, such as basic cables and lace, simple intarsia, double-pointed needles and knitting in the round needle techniques, mid-level shaping and finishing.
■■■■ EXPERIENCED	Projects using advanced techniques and stitches, such as short rows, fair isle, more intricate intarsia, cables, lace patterns, and numerous color changes.

INCREASE

Knit the next stitch but do **not** slip the old stitch off the left needle (*Fig. 1a*). Insert the right needle into the **back** loop of the **same** stitch and knit it (*Fig. 1b*), then slip the old stitch off the left needle.

Fig. 1a

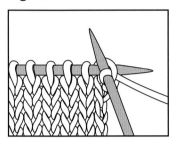

Fig. 1b

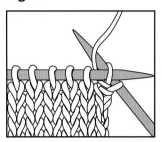

YARN OVERS

After a knit stitch, before a knit stitch

Bring the yarn forward **between** the needles, then back **over** the top of the right hand needle, so that it is now in position to knit the next stitch (Fig. 2a).

Fig. 2a

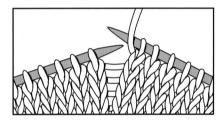

After a purl stitch, before a purl stitch

Take the yarn **over** the right hand needle to the back, then forward **under** it, so that it is now in position to purl the next stitch (Fig. 2b).

Fig. 2b

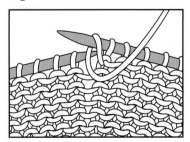

MAKE ONE (*abbreviated M1*)

Insert the **left** needle under the horizontal strand between the stitches from the front (*Fig. 3a*). Then knit into the **back** of the strand (*Fig. 3b*).

Fig. 3a

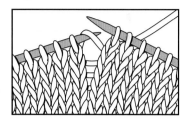

Fig. 3b

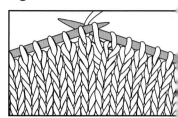

KNIT 2 TOGETHER (*abbreviated K2 tog*)

Insert the right needle into the **front** of the first two stitches on the left needle as if to **knit** (*Fig. 4*), then **knit** them together as if they were one stitch.

Fig. 4

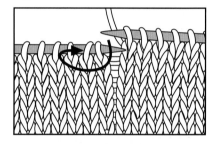

PURL 2 TOGETHER (*abbreviated P2 tog*)

Insert the right needle into the **front** of the first two stitches on the left needle as if to **purl** (*Fig. 5*), then **purl** them together as if they were one stitch.

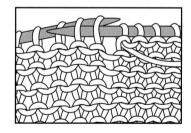